THE LITTLE BLACK BOOK FOR STUNNING SUCCESS

ROBIN SHARMA

JAICO PUBLISHING HOUSE

Ahmedabad Bangalore Bhopal Bhubaneswar Chennai
Delhi Hyderabad Kolkata Lucknow Mumbai

Published by Jaico Publishing House
A-2 Jash Chambers, 7-A Sir Phirozshah Mehta Road
Fort, Mumbai - 400 001
jaicopub@jaicobooks.com
www.jaicobooks.com

© Robin Sharma

Published in arrangement with
Sharma Leadership International Inc.
92 Scollard Street, 2nd Floor
Toronto, ON M5R 1G2, Canada

To be sold only in India, Bangladesh, Bhutan,
Pakistan, Nepal, Sri Lanka and the Maldives.

THE LITTLE BLACK BOOK FOR
STUNNING SUCCESS
ISBN 978-81-8495-989-5

First Jaico Impression: 2017
Eighth Jaico Impression: 2019

Page design and layout: Special Effects, Mumbai

Printed by
Rashmi Graphics
#3, Amrutwel CHS Ltd., C.S. #50/74
Ganesh Galli, Lalbaug, Mumbai - 400 012
E-mail: rashmigraphics84@gmail.com

CONTENTS

1

WHAT IS LEADERSHIP?

Leadership has nothing to do with the title on your business card or the size of your office. Leadership is not about how much money you make or the clothes you wear. Leadership is a philosophy. It's an attitude. It's a state of mind. And it's available to each one of us.

Here's an example. I spend a lot of my life traveling so I'm hard on my luggage. The handle on my carry-on luggage broke after my tour of Russia a few months ago (you have to put St. Petersburg on your list of places to visit before you die). Anyway, I took the piece in to Evex, a dealer in Toronto. The young man at the counter treated me wonderfully and within a few days, the handle was fixed.

While in New York a week ago, the handle broke again. I

assumed that I'd have to pay for the repair when I went back into Evex. Most businesses put clients through so many hurdles: if you haven't saved the receipt you are out of luck, if you don't know who did the initial repair we cannot help you, etc, etc. Well, Evex is different. They just get it. They understand that without treating their customers well, there will be no business.

When I explained that the handle broke again, the young woman at the counter, without a moment of hesitation, apologized for the problem I faced. She then said, "We will promise you that you will have your carry-on in perfect order within three days. And of course sir, there will be no charge." No bureaucracy around needing the receipt from the previous repair. No hassles. No issues. Just great service, with a giant smile.

This woman showed leadership. She quickly diagnosed the problem, assumed personal responsibility and made the right decision. And she wowed her customer in the process.

What will you do today to be the leader that you are destined to be?

LEADERSHIP IS A
PHILOSOPHY.
IT'S A MENTALITY.
IT'S A STATE OF
MIND.
IT'S A WAY OF
OPERATING.
AND IT'S
AVAILABLE TO
EACH
ONE
OF US.

What I'm Grateful for Today:

I'm grateful that I am healthy and still breathing. I am grateful that I have house to live in, food to eat and nice clothes to wear. I am grateful of the people I have in my life specially my grandparents.

Where I will Pursue Mastery Today:

Journal,
BOOKS
Music.
Spend time with family and myself,
less use of social media.

What I Learned Today:

When I was coming back home I realized one thing, everything I did in post, of the way I was always holding on to things, it was for happiness. All i did was to make myself happy and we don't have to be people pleser to make ourself happy.

2

WORLD-CLASS LANGUAGE

Language offers a framework for meaning. Think about that powerful idea for a second. We understand the world through words. The words you use determine the way you perceive reality.

If you call a stumbling block a "problem" or "a big mess", you will create a different emotional state within you than if you call the issue "an opportunity" or "a challenge that will only make me better".

I have the privilege, as a success coach, to work with many extraordinarily successful people from around the world.

One of their common traits of greatness is that the vast majority of them understand the power of the word. **They use world-class language.**

Not only do they refrain from using profanity, but they use the language of passion. They use the language of leadership. They use the language of possibility. They use the language of love.

INSIDE EVERY PROBLEM LIES A PRECIOUS OPPORTUNITY TO IMPROVE THINGS.

What I'm Grateful for Today:

— having family with me.

Where I will Pursue Mastery Today:

What I Learned Today:

3

WHO MADE SUCCESS
A BAD WORD?

Too many people believe that there's something wrong with aiming to be really successful. I've been hearing it a lot these days, the suggestion that if you strive for success, you must not be all that concerned with making a difference and being significant.

It's almost as if being a go-getter is incompatible with being compassionate, socially conscious and good.

Well here's my take on the 'success versus significance' issue: an extraordinary life contains both.

Without success, I have a sense that the best part of you will feel a little hollow.

Part of what makes us human is the hunger to realize our greatest gifts and live life fully. We were built to shine. And without significance, I believe that we will feel that we have walked the planet in vain.

There's nothing wrong with being an elite performer and taking the steps required to become a remarkable success in this world.

Success is actually a creative pursuit and a reflection of healthy self-esteem.

And while you realize success, I urge you to stay devoted to elevating the lives you touch and leaving your world better than you found it.

That's the significance piece. With both, you'll discover your greatest life.

TO BE A LEADER
IS NOT TO HAVE
A HUGE
POSITION.
TO BE A LEADER
IS TO SEE YOUR
JOB AS A
CHANCE
TO IMPACT THE
WORLD,
NO MATTER
WHAT YOUR
JOB IS.

What I'm Grateful for Today:

Where I will Pursue Mastery Today:

What I Learned Today:

4

THE POWER OF DAILY PRACTICES

Success, world-class health, internal fulfillment and sustained happiness don't just happen. These elements of your best life are created.

All too often we look at a human being playing their best game on the playing field of life and assume they got lucky or were born into their lofty condition.

What we don't see is all the devotion and discipline that went into crafting the extraordinary results we see.

What I'm suggesting is that personal and professional greatness takes work. I'm not someone who would ever tell you that you could get to your dreams without having to make some sacrifices and pay the price in terms of dedication and self-control.

The best amongst us make it all look so easy. I call it **The Swan Effect** – elite performers making personal excellence look effortless and things happen as gracefully as a swan moving along the water.

But like the swan, what you don't get to see is all the hard-work taking place below the surface.

The best way to create spectacular results in the most important areas of your life is through daily practice.

In my life, I have a series of practices that set me up for a great day.

Yes, sometimes life sends you unexpected challenges that knock you off track – that's just life happening. But with a series of practices to keep you at your best, you'll stay in a positive state much more often.

Practices that will lock you into your best state include a **morning journaling session** where you record your feelings, thoughts and the blessings you are grateful for.

Or you may start your day with a strong workout and an elite performer's meal.

I often **listen to music for 15 minutes**, as it not only energizes me but also just makes life better. I also **use success statements or affirmations** to get my mind focused.

Success and joy and inner peace don't just show up. You need to create them.

Find your series of practices, perform them with consistency. And then, go out into this beautiful world of ours and shine.

HUGE
ACHIEVEMENT
IS LESS ABOUT
YOUR
GENETICS
AND MORE ABOUT
YOUR
RITUALS.

What I'm Grateful for Today:

_____

_____

_____

_____

_____

_____

Where I will Pursue Mastery Today:

_____

_____

_____

_____

_____

What I Learned Today:

_____

_____

_____

_____

_____

_____

5

THE EYES OF LEADERSHIP

The sad fact is that most people see the worst in others. They see others through the eyes of their own anger, fear and limitation. If someone shows up late for a meeting, they impute a negative intent on that person, saying, "They are so rude".

If someone makes a mistake on an expense report, they grumble, "That person is so dishonest". If someone mis-communicates a point, they silently say, "She's a liar".

Leaders are different.

They look for the best in people. I want to be clear. I'm not suggesting that leaders do not confront reality. Not at all. What I'm saying is that **the best leaders see through the eyes of understanding.**

If someone is late, they try to get to the truth. Maybe there's a time management problem to coach around or a sick child to help. An error on an expense account could be the result of a poor process in place or the employee's disorganization. The miscommunication might be all about the person communicating having weak skills in this area. Maybe there is an opportunity for improvement.

Today, rather than looking for the worst in people, I invite you to look for what's best within them.

Sure, some people really are inconsiderate or dishonest or uncaring. But in my experience – and I've worked with a lot of people over the years – most people are good.

Few human beings wake up in the morning and ask themselves: "What can I do today to mess up someone else's day or undermine my credibility?"

Most of the mistakes people make are the result of a lack of awareness. And here's the payoff for you: as you seek out the good in people, not only will they want to show up more fully for you, but you will see more good in your world.

THE PURER THE STREAM, THE BETTER THE WATER. THE GREATER THE LEADER, THE MORE SUCCESSFUL THE FIRM.

What I'm Grateful for Today:

_____

_____

_____

_____

_____

_____

_____

Where I will Pursue Mastery Today:

_____

_____

_____

_____

_____

_____

What I Learned Today:

_____

_____

_____

_____

_____

_____

6

THE MYTH OF PERSONAL TRANSFORMATION

Too many people believe that playing their best game as a human being requires them to revolutionize their lives. And for most of us, that's a scary thought.

No one wants to make massive changes to the way they think, feel and behave.

Human beings love staying within their comfort zone.

But guess what?

In my work as a success coach with people around the world, I've realized that lasting personal change does not require you to turn your life upside down.

The best way to get to your greatness is through small, continuous steps – what I call the '1% Wins'.

If you improve your health by only 1% each day for the next 30 days, you will see a 30% increase in that dimension of your life in only one month.

The same goes for every other area of your life, from your relationships to your career.

Doesn't seem so scary now, does it? Can you make those little improvements in the areas most in need of improvement? Absolutely.

WITHOUT PATIENCE, THERE CAN BE NO GENIUS.

What I'm Grateful for Today:

Where I will Pursue Mastery Today:

What I Learned Today:

7

LIVE FULLY, NOW

Too many human beings postpone living.

We say that we will live our best lives when we have more time or when we finish the pressing projects that are consuming us.

We tell those around us that we will be more loving and passionate when things slow down.

We promise ourselves that we will get into world-class physical condition and eat healthier food when we have a little more time.

Yet, deep within, each one of us knows that there will never be a better time to live our biggest life than now.

And if not today, then when?

MAKE A STOP-DOING LIST SO YOU DELETE THE MISUSE OF YOUR OH-SO-PRECIOUS TIME.

What I'm Grateful for Today:

_____

_____

_____

_____

_____

_____

Where I will Pursue Mastery Today:

_____

_____

_____

_____

_____

_____

What I Learned Today:

_____

_____

_____

_____

_____

_____

8

SIMPLIFY, THEN FOCUS

Henry David Thoreau shouted "Simplify. Simplify. Simplify", in his breathtakingly good book *Walden*. Nice point.

One of the primary reasons that people and organizations fail to achieve greatness is that they try to be too many things to too many people.

Here, I'll use the Confucius quote I often use: "Man who chases two rabbits catches neither."

The most successful human beings are wildly focused. They have a very clear picture of what it is they want to create by the time they reach the end of their lives and then they have the discipline (and courage) to stick to their mission, saying "no" to everything that is not mission critical.

So my gentle suggestion to you is – simplify your life. Strip away all that is unimportant – these are the things keeping you from getting to your dreams. And then, once you do your clean up – focus, focus, focus. You'll be surprised how good you will then get at being great.

**LESS EXCUSES,
MORE RESULTS.
LESS DISTRACTIONS,
MORE FOCUS.
LESS ME,
MORE WE.**

What I'm Grateful for Today:

Where I will Pursue Mastery Today:

What I Learned Today:

9

HOW TO GET GOOD AT LIFE

Life is a skill. And like any other skill, once you know the ground rules and make the time to practice, you can get better. If you really devote yourself to life, you could even reach a place of mastery. Some have.

I suggest to you the three simple things you can do to get good at life:

1. **Pay Attention to Life:** It's really easy to let life act on you; to fall asleep to life. Some people have lost entire decades this way. And they never got them back. Try and write in a journal each morning before you walk out into your world. Think about what goals you need to accomplish that day and write them down. Think about

what your most closely held values are. Think about what lessons you've learned from the previous day. What good is making a mistake if you don't learn from it?

2. **Engage in Life:** I've learned something as I've grown older – the more you give to life, the more it gives to you. Over dinner last night with some friends, we began to speak of goal setting. "But why set goals when life can be so uncertain?" one asked me. My reply: "Just because life is so unpredictable doesn't mean you shouldn't exercise your power to do your best. Set your goals. Make your plans. Take action and chase your dreams. That's what personal responsibility is all about. But once you've done your best, let go. And let life do the rest." She looked deeply into her pad Thai.

3. **Enjoy Life:** We take life too seriously. But at the end, the billionaire gets buried next to the street sweeper. We all end up as dust.

And no matter how long you live, none of us are here for all that long in the grand scheme of things.

So let's not take ourselves too seriously.

Let's enjoy the ride.

SMILE. DREAM.
LOVE. LEARN.
PUSH. REST.
CREATE. DRIVE.
LISTEN. BREATHE.
HUG. EXCEL.
WIN. LOSE.
BE. DO.
LIVE.

What I'm Grateful for Today:

_____

_____

_____

_____

_____

_____

Where I will Pursue Mastery Today:

_____

_____

_____

_____

_____

_____

What I Learned Today:

_____

_____

_____

_____

_____

_____

10

YOUR FOUR-MINUTE MILE

The philosopher Arthur Schopenhauer once observed: "Most people take the limits of their vision to be the limits of the world. A few do not. Join them."

Profound point. The life you see this very moment isn't necessarily the life of your future. You might be viewing things through the eyes of your fears, limitations and false assumptions.

Once you clean up the stained glass window you see the world through... guess what? A whole new set of possibilities appear.

Remember, we see the world not as it is but as we are.

That idea changed my life.

Years ago, it was believed that no human being could ever

break the 4-minute mile barrier. But after Roger Bannister broke it, many more replicated his feat within weeks.

Why?

Because he showed people what was possible. And then armed with that belief, people did the impossible.

What's your '4-minute mile'? What bill of goods have you sold yourself as to what's impossible?

What false assumptions are you making in terms of what you cannot have, do and be?

Your thinking creates your reality.

If you think something cannot occur in your life, then there's no way you will take the action required to make that goal a reality.

Your 'impossibility thinking' becomes a self-fulfilling prophecy.

Your perceived limitations become the chains that keep you from the greatness you were meant to be. And where's the leadership in that?

IN A WORLD THAT **REVERES** SUPERFICIALITY, **GO DEEP.** IN A WORLD THAT **HONOURS** DISTRACTION, **BE FOCUSED.** IN A WORLD THAT **SUGGESTS** SELFISHNESS, **SERVE.** THIS IS HOW YOU RISE TO BE LEGENDARY.

What I'm Grateful for Today:

Where I will Pursue Mastery Today:

What I Learned Today:

11

CALL YOUR PARENTS, KISS YOUR SPOUSE AND HUG YOUR KIDS

Ever notice that it's the people we love most that we most take for granted? Odd isn't it. It's easy to spend less time with your family because they will always be there for you (or so you assume). It's easy to put off expressing your love to your loved ones because there seems to be no urgency at play. It's easy to let home relationships slip because you assume there are more pressing things to deal with.

But what could possibly be more important than your family? Is there any wisdom in being successful, yet alone?

So pick up the phone and tell your parents that you love them. Before you leave for work, give your spouse a kiss, like you mean it.

And please, please, please, hug your kids. Enjoy them while

you can – they'll only be young once. And once that window of opportunity closes, it will be gone forever.

UNDERSTAND THAT
EVERY PERSON
WHO HAS SHOWN UP
IN YOUR LIFE
ARRIVED TO
HELP YOU
BECOME THE
PERSON
YOU NOW ARE.
APPRECIATE AND
LOVE THEM.

What I'm Grateful for Today:

Where I will Pursue Mastery Today:

What I Learned Today:

12

NO TRAIN, NO GAIN

What do The Ritz Carlton, The Hotel Victor (in Miami), Nike, Amazon, Omni Health Care, IBM, KPMG and other organizations that consistently deliver near-flawless execution of world-class customer service have in common?

Their management understands that money spent on training is not an expense – it's an investment.

If your greatest resource is your people (and who wouldn't agree with that?), then it only makes sense that your biggest investment should be in your people.

Developing them. Growing them. Training them.

In economically hard times, what's the first thing short-sighted companies cut? You guessed it – the training budget. Unbelievable. What message does that send to people?

Spectacular success in business doesn't come by luck.

The best companies didn't get to their lofty positions by chance. The great ones didn't reach the mountaintop by coincidence.

They got there by relentlessly focusing on the right things. Like delivering outrageous value to their customers. Like innovating as if there's no tomorrow.

And by investing in the human beings who are at the heart and soul of the enterprise.

How easy it is to forget that the true worth of your organization walks in through the front doors of your building every morning and leaves through them every night.

No train, no gain.

IDEAS
DON'T WORK
WITHOUT YOU
DOING THE
WORK.

What I'm Grateful for Today:

Where I will Pursue Mastery Today:

What I Learned Today:

13

DETACH FROM
THE NOISE

One of the primary traits of world-class performers (in business and in life) is their ability to 'detach from the noise'. Each day, 'noise' such as little crises, minor interruptions and interesting distractions beg for our attention. To get to your own unique form of personal and professional greatness, it's important – no, essential – to detach from the noise and stay 'on vision'.

A simple daily practice to keep you on course to get to your dreams is spending a period immersed in silence each morning.

Before your day gets noisy, close your eyes and reflect on your mission. Think about your goals. Reflect on what are your most important To-Dos today. Those things that will get you to your dreams.

We all face 'the tyranny of the urgent' during our days. But the best of the best stay true to their vision, values and virtues. And they ensure that the things that truly count never get sacrificed for those seemingly pressing but unimportant ones. They simply refuse to major in the minor. They avoid the noise.

IT WILL BE
HARD.
YOU WILL GET
HURT.
PEOPLE WILL BE
JEALOUS.
YOU WILL WANT TO
QUIT.
YOU WILL
KEEP ON.
IT WILL BE
WORTH IT.
YOU WILL
WIN.

What I'm Grateful for Today:

_____

_____

_____

_____

_____

_____

Where I will Pursue Mastery Today:

_____

_____

_____

_____

_____

_____

What I Learned Today:

_____

_____

_____

_____

_____

_____

14

YOU BE ENTHUSIASTIC

"Be Enthusiastic" smacks of trite sloganeering. "Be energetic" sounds obvious. "Be passionate" seems boring. Yet without enthusiasm, energy and passion, you cannot lead your field and an organization cannot get to world-class. (Hey, I never pretended this leadership stuff was rocket science.)

The people I love to be around are often those that have a simple, heartfelt quality – they are enthusiastic.

They are open to life. They are curious. They love to learn. They smile when they see me. And they have a lot of fun.

Today, show up at work with all the enthusiasm you can genuinely muster.

See the best in people.
Go the extra mile to wow your customers.
See the opportunity amidst a seeming setback.
Embrace change as an opportunity to grow.
Learn something new.
Have a laugh with a teammate.

I'll be the first to agree that you can't control what happens to you each day. But with an abundance of enthusiasm, I have no doubt that whatever the coming hours bring, you will handle them with grace, strength and a smile.

WORLD-BUILDERS CAN LIVE WITH FAILURE. THEY JUST CAN'T LIVE WITH NOT TRYING.

What I'm Grateful for Today:

_____

_____

_____

_____

_____

_____

Where I will Pursue Mastery Today:

_____

_____

_____

_____

_____

What I Learned Today:

_____

_____

_____

_____

_____

_____

15

WHY THOUGHTS SHAPE REALITY

You've heard it a thousand times in a thousand different ways: you become what you think about. And the thoughts you use become self-fulfilling prophecies. Expect extraordinary things to unfold for you, and they will.

The motivators say it. The teachers say it. The sages say it. Ever wonder why? I think I finally understand why the idea is truth. It's not some esoteric philosophy. It's simple logic. Here we go:

The actions you take each day create the results of your life. And since every action you take has been preceded by a thought (thinking truly is the ancestor of performance), what you focus on does drive your reality.

British Prime Minister Bejamin Disrael said it so well when

he observed, "You will never go higher than your thinking." A human being will never act in a way bigger than his thoughts. Dream big and your behavior will follow. Think small and you'll play small.

This concept cascades throughout every dimension of our lives.

Think people are good and you walk through your days with an open heart. And that behavior actually becomes your reality because people do good things for good people.

Think you deserve the best and your actions will reflect that confidence. Better actions will then drive better results.

Expect to be one of the great ones in your career or within your country. That brilliant thinking shapes the way you work and the way you show up in general. And that world-class conduct presents world-class outcomes.

I hope I've expressed the point clearly. It's a big idea that is so easy to neglect as obvious. Your thoughts shape your reality. Your thinking forms your world. What you focus on expands. And what you dwell on determines your destiny.

WHEN YOUR HEART IS BROKEN, IT IS MOST OPEN. WHEN LIFE HAS CRUSHED YOUR DREAMS, IT HAS PRODUCED A PATH TOWARD EVEN BETTER ONES. BE NOT DISCOURAGED. YOU'RE BUILT TO WIN.

MY ACTION MASTERY TOOL

What I'm Grateful for Today:

_____

_____

_____

_____

_____

Where I will Pursue Mastery Today:

_____

_____

_____

_____

_____

What I Learned Today:

_____

_____

_____

_____

_____

16

IT ONLY TAKES
A MINUTE

It only takes a minute to tell a loved one you adore them.

It only takes a minute to run towards a fear.

It only takes a minute to set a big goal.

It only takes a minute to drink a glass of water.

It only takes a minute to read a great idea (that just might rock your world).

It only takes a minute to write the most beautiful Thank You note you have ever sent your parents (or a teammate or a customer or a high school teacher who blessed your life).

It only takes a minute to smile.

It only takes a minute to connect to a friend or a co-worker.

It only takes a minute to help a human being in need.

It only takes a minute to raise your standards to world-class.

It only takes a minute to go the extra mile at work and wow a customer.

It only takes a minute to reflect on what you can do today to be better than you were yesterday.

It only takes a minute to embrace change.

It only takes a minute to make a new choice that will lead to your best life.

Make the best of your minutes. Each one of them makes up your life.

THE HOURS THAT ORDINARY PEOPLE WASTE, EXTRAORDINARY PEOPLE LEVERAGE.

What I'm Grateful for Today:

Where I will Pursue Mastery Today:

What I Learned Today:

17

TELL GREAT STORIES

Big Idea: People step into the stories you create for them. People generally behave in a way that meets the expectations you have of them. People generally conduct themselves in alignment with the belief, faith and trust you've developed around them. And they mostly behave in accordance with the tightly cherished perceptions that you've structured about them.

Tell your kid that she's your hero each morning and that kid is going to shine like the North Star for the rest of her life (tell your kids they're amazing at least 500 times a day and hug them like you'll never see them again).

Tell your teammate that you wish you were half as good as them and you've just created a space of possibility for that human being to step into (and up to).

Tell the person who serves you your next restaurant meal that you appreciate them and then flash the most honest smile you can muster (doesn't matter if you're tired – leaders do what's right versus easy). Do so and you've just reminded a human to be human and spread some of your stardust (and you might just get a free meal).

Tell good stories.

For every person you meet, suggest (by your words, your tone, your behavior and your energy) that you have a story deep in your mind of how great they are.

See the best in people.

Look for greatness inside them.

Remind people that they were meant to shine by the stories you tell them.

Stories about their magnificence.

YOU CAN'T INSPIRE PEOPLE IF YOU HAVE NO INSPIRATION. SO START DOING THINGS EACH DAY THAT FILL YOU WITH INSPIRATION. AND THEN YOU'LL INSPIRE.

What I'm Grateful for Today:

Where I will Pursue Mastery Today:

What I Learned Today:

18

ASK, ASK, ASK... THEN ASK SOME MORE

You'll never know if you don't even try. There is giant power in asking for what you want. All too often, our internal chatter prevents us from taking the steps needed to get us to our own unique form of greatness.

We get kept small by our inner imaginings – so many of which are lies.

The best of the best, those who live glorious lives, that matter, ask like crazy.

They understand that asking questions is a habit that must be polished for it to shine. And the more you do it, the easier it gets (like any skill).

And so they ask. For the support and help they need at work. For the understanding they may seek at home. For a break they need for their business. For a better table at their favorite restaurant.

For a better seat at a sold-out concert.

And because they ask more, they get more (success always has been a numbers game).

Nothing happens until you ask. People are not mind readers. They need to know what's meaningful to you, and if you ask nicely, they just might say yes.

NOTHING HAPPENS UNTIL YOU MOVE. NOTHING TRANSFORMS UNTIL YOU EXECUTE.

What I'm Grateful for Today:

Where I will Pursue Mastery Today:

What I Learned Today:

19

DO GOOD
TO FEEL GOOD

It is so easy to forget this one: doing good makes you feel good. Being kind to a co-worker not only enables and elevates their mood – it lifts yours too. Adding outrageous value to a customer and making him feel like the VIP that he is not only makes him your goodwill ambassador (spreading word of your services like a virus), it unlocks a wellspring of positive sensations inside of you. Going the extra mile for your spouse or your child not only leaves them better than you found them, it helps you feel connected to the ones you love (which promotes happiness and fulfillment).

Not only do good things happen to good people (life's got this really fair accounting system; Nature must have an MBA in accounting), but people who do great things get to feel great feelings.

This isn't some "soft" idea (and if ideas like these are so "soft" why are they so very hard to do? Anyone can be cranky or unkind or mediocre. Being positive and kind and excellent takes a lot more discipline and power).

No, this thought I'm sharing isn't "soft" at all. It's a practical, powerful insight that will lead you to real results – in your business life. In your personal life. And in your inner life.

Do good for people. Do good work. Think good thoughts. And be good to yourself. Good things will happen.

Okay, I'll stop using the word 'good' now... it's just that it feels so... good.

BETTER TO BE AN OPTIMIST WHO GETS DISAPPOINTED THAN A PESSIMIST WHO HAS NO HOPE.

What I'm Grateful for Today:

Where I will Pursue Mastery Today:

What I Learned Today:

20

FIND POCKETS
OF PEACE

It is a noisy world we live in. People talk loudly on cell phones. Ring tones can be heard in once serene restaurants. Most cars have radios on. Most homes have TVs on. I saw a man chatting on his Blackberry while eating his oatmeal yesterday. Not good for digestion.

Each of us, I suggest, must find 'pockets of peace'. Time for what I call 'The 3 Ss':

Silence, Solitude and Stillness.

At least, find some time (say 15 minutes a day) to be quiet.

Think. Reflect. Be.

That best practice will make you much better at work, at

home and with your self.

Some Practical Strategies:

- When you are in your car or in a taxi, keep the radio off. Use that time to renew. To observe. To introspect.

- Take 15 minutes before you sleep to immerse yourself in peace. Just chill. Get comfortable with no noise. Get comfortable with yourself.

- Make your home a sanctuary. It's a wild world (jungle?) out there. Create a deeply peaceful home environment. Reduce clutter. Cut back on the noise. Get one of those mobile water fountains.

- Take a daily vow of silence.

This one isn't just for monks. It's for smart executives, entrepreneurs, businesspeople. Big idea here: talking consumes a ton of energy. I can't believe how much some people talk. All day long – on their mobiles, at the water cooler and on the train home. It is exhausting just to watch them. Be silent for 15 minutes a day (at the very least). You'll have more energy. More peace. More joy. And so, better performance.

So chase – no, hunt peace down. Fight the noise. Get away from the maddening crowds, at least for a bit. You'll be glad you did.

THE IDEA ISN'T TO STRUGGLE THROUGH LIFE. THE MINDSET IS TO CREATE + GROW + LOVE + SERVE THROUGH LIFE.

MY ACTION MASTERY TOOL

What I'm Grateful for Today:

_____

_____

_____

_____

_____

_____

_____

Where I will Pursue Mastery Today:

_____

_____

_____

_____

_____

_____

_____

What I Learned Today:

_____

_____

_____

_____

_____

_____

21

THIS DAY IS SPECIAL

I'm up early. Drinking coffee. Listening to Morcheeba. Writing in my journal, about where I'm at in my life, as I close in on 52. About what I'm grateful for (for example, people like you who allow me to do what I do – thank you). About what needs to get done in the coming days, weeks, months or years for me to feel like I've made my impact and done my dream.

Then an insight surfaced that I need to share with you.

The compelling idea: this day is so very special.

Sure, it arrives like all the others, looks the same and might even feel the same. But it is unique. It'll never come again.

Time is like that, comes full of promise and leaves before you know it.

What you do between today's sunrise and sunset is creating

your destiny, your future and your legacy. And a single choice you make today can change your life over the coming months if consistently acted upon.

Spoke to a friend last night. He said something I slept on: "My wife's God is money. My God is time."

I get what he meant; he knows time is the scarcest resource. Use it well and life sends you the extraordinary. Waste it and your heart feels empty. And your life looks hollow.

This day is special. Honor it. Do something great today. I know you can.

Will you?

STRESS ISN'T THE PROBLEM. A LACK OF REFUELLING FROM STRESS IS WHAT REDUCES PERFORMANCE. EPIC PRODUCERS WORK HARD. AND THEN HAVE FUN.

What I'm Grateful for Today:

_____

_____

_____

_____

_____

Where I will Pursue Mastery Today:

_____

_____

_____

_____

_____

What I Learned Today:

_____

_____

_____

_____

_____

22

FEAR AS GROWTH

Fear can be scary. When it surfaces, we are wired to run. To avoid it. To consider it as a bad thing. Not true. In my mind fear is beautiful. An opportunity. A gift.

On the other side of every fear that is keeping you small is your natural power (and your authentic greatness). To run from your fear is to run from the brilliance you were meant to be. A fear is nothing more than a doorway into the highest version of your highest vision. The things that scare you are spectacular opportunities to discover more of all you are meant to be. Fear isn't bad. It is in fact all good. Leads to confidence (if you do what you fear). Leads to self-respect. Promotes growth. Makes you better.

So today, at work or at home, if something comes up that

causes you to feel like running, avoiding or even resisting, don't make a beeline for the door.

Instead, show up like the leader you truly can be – and embrace the opportunity you've been presented. Because what you resist will persist. But what you befriend, you'll transcend.

IF YOU'RE NOT SCARED A LOT, YOU'RE NOT GROWING VERY MUCH.

What I'm Grateful for Today:

_____

_____

_____

_____

_____

_____

Where I will Pursue Mastery Today:

_____

_____

_____

_____

_____

_____

What I Learned Today:

_____

_____

_____

_____

_____

_____

23

PRACTICE THE LARRY KING RULE

I remember watching CNN talk show host Larry King being interviewed on PBS by Charlie Rose. He said something that I've carried with me to this day. A simple point (like the best points):

Work out first thing in the morning, then what should get done will get done.

Perfect. Health is your wealth. Without it, you have nothing. You know that. Do you live that though?

I had coffee with an amazing friend and thinker last week. He's in his early forties and operates at a rare level of fitness. "Robin, my philosophy is that the way I treat my body now determines whether I'll be healthy or sick when I'm seventy." Brilliant insight. And he works out in the morning.

So here are the seven reasons to exercise in the morning that I teach my executive coaching clients as well as the organizations we work with, to unleash the potential of their people:

1. As Larry King suggested, if you work out early, it just gets done. Otherwise, it's so easy to come up with excuses not to work out as your day unfolds (hungry, tired, stressed out and need to go home to my family or tomorrow will be a better day to do it).

2. By working out in the morning, you actually jump start your metabolism and start up your fat burning engine within. So your workout has an even greater impact and more leverage.

3. By working out in the morning, you'll make better choices around your diet. Isn't that true? When we feel fit, we eat better.

4. The burst of energy that an early morning workout provokes will sustain you and keep you energized all day. It increases your stamina.

5. The endorphin rush that your morning workout generates makes you feel happy – which carries through each of your day's remaining hours (that alone is worth it; there IS a "secret" to happiness. Cost: A pair of running shoes).

6. An early morning workout burns off your stress. And, it increases your perspective. Problems just don't seem as big. And creativity soars. You can handle the day with far greater focus, resilience to change and calmness.

7. The morning workout will help you to think more clearly. As the best businesspeople are those who are the best thinkers (and decision makers).

So join me. Please. Get up early and exercise. Simple idea. That just might revolutionize your career as well as your life.

TODAY'S A GREAT DAY TO BEHAVE AS THE PERSON YOU HAVE ALWAYS WANTED TO BE.

MY ACTION MASTERY TOOL

What I'm Grateful for Today:

Where I will Pursue Mastery Today:

What I Learned Today:

24

SELL GREATLY

I just had an encounter with a salesperson I'll never see again. He wasn't rude. He wasn't incompetent. He wasn't uncaring. He was okay on every front. But in a world with a dazzling array of choices as to who we can give our business to, I opt for dealing with salespeople and organizations who are great.

Here's what happened...

Looking for a new laptop. I walk in and find the first person I see. He's plugging away on his computer. Says "Hi", without looking up (I'm serious). I try and engage him. He eventually tears himself away from the screen to look at the human being standing in front of him.

He answers some of my questions.

Begrudgingly.

He shows me some of his wares and essentially struggles to do what he's paid to get done, while giving a monologue on why I should buy what he's selling.

I went to his competitor across the street. They treat me beautifully – they get it. They got my business too.

I've worked with a lot of sales teams over the years, as a speaker and as a leadership coach.

Some quick observations from the best:

- Use people's names
- Look them in the eye and show them you care
- Say please and thank you
- Listen a thousand times more than you speak (only a slight exaggeration)
- Be on time
- Keep your promises
- Be more concerned about helping than selling (people can sniff sincerity from a mile away)
- Be passionate about your products and services so that passion gets transferred (the first sales person had all the passion of an old shoe box)
- Be better than anyone else in your field at what you do (so read up on the product, learn daily, develop yourself and your skills and always be improving)
- Treat your customers like they are visiting royalty

Simple strategies. But remember: what separates the best from the rest is their consistent adherence to a few simple practices that over time evolve into spectacular results.

And also remember, everyone is selling something.

IN YOUR BUSINESS, TAKE CARE OF YOUR RELATIONSHIPS AND MONEY WILL TAKE CARE OF ITSELF.

What I'm Grateful for Today:

_____

_____

_____

_____

_____

_____

Where I will Pursue Mastery Today:

_____

_____

_____

_____

_____

What I Learned Today:

_____

_____

_____

_____

_____

25

KUDOS TO WARREN BUFFET

Love it. The world's second richest man, Warren Buffett, just earmarked over $30 billion to donate to the charity of the world's richest man, Bill Gates, and his wife Melinda. Social responsibility is alive and well.

There is hope on our small planet.

The New Breed of Leaders understand that there's nothing wrong with making money. They get that building a highly profitable (and excellent) organization is part of the great game of business (and definitely one way to keep score).

But they also appreciate that with rewards comes responsibility.

And so they work hard to build an enterprise that is good. And honorable. And one that makes a positive difference in this world we are stewards of.

So a gigantic kudos to Warren Buffett. And to Bill and Melinda Gates (whose foundation is making important strides in the war against HIV and malaria).

And to all those other leaders who not only take care of themselves but use their gifts to elevate others. You inspire us. And you make a difference.

BEING KIND AND GRACIOUS AS A HUMAN DOESN'T MEAN BEING WEAK AND PATHETIC. JUST MEANS YOU'RE KIND AND GRACIOUS.

What I'm Grateful for Today:

_____

_____

_____

_____

_____

_____

Where I will Pursue Mastery Today:

_____

_____

_____

_____

_____

What I Learned Today:

_____

_____

_____

_____

_____

_____

26

WHY BE GREAT

Sure it takes effort, discipline and gigantic focus to get to world-class (and live your greatest life). Sure leadership is about doing what's right versus easy. And I agree that success requires sacrifices. So why do it? Because it'll make you feel good. Which makes it all worthwhile.

The big idea: Playing below your potential makes you feel bad about yourself. Operating below your potential diminishes your self-respect. Limiting what you can do, be or have sucks the energy out of your spirit and knocks the passion out of your heart.

Climbing your personal and professional mountaintop makes you feel good about yourself. Boost your self-respect. Heighten your self-image. This fills you with energy, faith and joy.

Achieving superb things with the gifts that are within you is one of the best ways to fill your life with more happiness. Being great – even when it's not easy to do so – is a brilliant move. That yields handsome rewards. Always.

NOT UNDERSTANDING IS THE BEGINNING OF LEARNING. CONFUSION IS A REFLECTION OF GROWTH. KEEP MOVING FORWARD. GREATNESS ADORES THE RELENTLESS.

What I'm Grateful for Today:

Where I will Pursue Mastery Today:

What I Learned Today:

27

ROUGH CONDITIONS BRING PRECIOUS GIFTS

Nature is an incredible teacher. Life is run by Nature's rules. So it only makes sense to observe how nature works to really get how life works.

This morning I observed something fascinating. The rains last night here in Southern Italy caused a little miracle on the verandah of the apartment we are staying at: the collection of cacti in the garden has morphed into a stunning array of flowers. I've never seen flowers blooming from cacti.

The Takeaway: Rough conditions can bring precious gifts.

Life can be hard. We all have our good seasons as well as our difficult ones. But hard times bring many blessings, like:

- Strength of character
- Self-knowledge
- Courage
- Greater understanding
- Deeper compassion

Some of the qualities of the very best leaders that have walked before us.

We grow the most as human beings during our roughest times. So why do we judge them as bad when they bring such good? The challenging pieces of our lives just might be when we are most alive. And, if you are awake to them, they always bring tiny miracles.

THE HARDER THE SITUATION, THE MORE GROWTH THERE IS AVAILABLE TO YOU IF YOU LOOK FOR IT.

What I'm Grateful for Today:

Where I will Pursue Mastery Today:

What I Learned Today:

28

YOUR ENVIRONMENT BECOMES YOU

You will become your surroundings. So choose them well.

The people you associate with and the conversations you have profoundly shape your thinking and actions.

Be with people greater than you and you will become a greater person.

Fill your home with great books and you will rise to meet the promise (and possibilities) they offer.

Eat great, healthy food and your physical life will reflect that association.

Place yourself in and around the best. And you'll become it.

SOMETIMES YOU NEED TO SLOW DOWN TO EVENTUALLY GO FASTER.

What I'm Grateful for Today:

Where I will Pursue Mastery Today:

What I Learned Today:

29

FAIL TO
WIN

The very nature of dreaming big dreams and stretching
yourself beyond the normal is dangerous.

Dangerous in the sense that you leave safety, you leave
routine, you leave the common world where unhappy people
smile giant smiles when they are asked to pose for a picture
(guess I'm feeling a little poetic on this hot summer's day).

And as you leave your cocoon of comfort, you will certainly
fail more than your neighbors and those who live a life called
Ordinary. But one must fail to win.

One must be willing to risk greatly to reach your personal
mountaintop and your authentic definition of success.

And I'd rather reach high and be disappointed than not
even try to reach. And when I fall, I get back up, dust myself

off – and I start again. Wiser, stronger and more committed. Just like you.

SOMETIMES WE NEED TO LOSE OUR WAY TO FIND OUR WAY.

What I'm Grateful for Today:

_____

_____

_____

_____

_____

_____

Where I will Pursue Mastery Today:

_____

_____

_____

_____

_____

_____

What I Learned Today:

_____

_____

_____

_____

_____

_____

30

THE IMAGINATION ECONOMY

We all know that ideas are the currency of success these days. To win in your marketspace, it's mission-critical to out-think, out-innovate and out-create your competition. The person with the biggest ideas blended with the best execution will lead the field.

This brings me to Ryanair. Ryanair is a VCC (Very Cool Company). It is Europe's most profitable airline (about $400 million in profit so far this year) at a time when other airlines are sinking with high fuel prices (JetBlue, another VCC that I used to rave about in my leadership presentations, lost money this year for the first time ever).

In the past 12 months Ryanair has flown 35 million passengers at an average ticket price of just over $50. And, get this, 25% of its flights are free. Seriously.

Billing itself as 'The Wal-Mart of Flying', Ryanair's goal is to one day (soon) make flying absolutely free.

So how does it make money?

By charging for other services. Advertising revenue comes from commercials on the back of seats. Checked luggage costs $3.50 per piece. Food is always extra.

By reinventing the business model for winning in their industry, Ryanair is doing just that. And showing us what innovation and imagination is all about in the change-crazy economy we find ourselves operating within.

IDEATION WITHOUT EXECUTION IS DELUSION.

What I'm Grateful for Today:

_____

_____

_____

_____

_____

_____

_____

Where I will Pursue Mastery Today:

_____

_____

_____

_____

_____

_____

What I Learned Today:

_____

_____

_____

_____

_____

_____

31

DON'T FEED YOUR WEAKNESS

A simple insight for you today: every time you practice a weakness, you feed it. And the things you feed grow in your life.

Every time you don't live your values, the Integrity Gap widens. Every time you run from a fear, the fear expands. Every time you mistreat another person, your capacity to mistreat becomes more powerful.

We become excellent by doing excellent things (over and over and over until they become a part of our wiring).

We become fearless by visiting the places that scare us.

We become strong by living our strengths, not our weaknesses.

JUST REMEMBER, YOU CAN'T WIN THE GAME IF YOU DON'T EVEN PLAY IT.

What I'm Grateful for Today:

Where I will Pursue Mastery Today:

What I Learned Today:

32

THE THING ABOUT THINGS

Here's the thing about spending your life or energy or talents chasing things: the more you get, the more you want. They never fulfill their promise of happiness. It's a pretty cruel ruse once you really think about it.

You get the car you've been dreaming of for years and after a few days, you're already thinking about the next one. You move into your dream home or get your dream job and within a couple of weeks, the attraction has faded and the sparkle has gone. It's no longer exciting. Your attention moves on to the next desire.

What life has taught me (and I'm certainly no guru and definitely don't have all the answers) is that **things can never bring you joy that lasts.**

I want to be incredibly clear: there's absolutely nothing wrong, in my mind, with having, collecting or wanting nice things. They make the climb to the mountaintop more pleasant.

I guess what I'm trying to say is that perhaps the key for us is not to worship them. Not to get hooked by them. Not to be enslaved by all things material. Enjoy them. Just don't get caught in the trap they often set.

So that begs the question: "Where does real and sustained joy or fulfillment come from?"

Here's a quick list based on my current level of understanding (Big idea: we cannot see any higher than the level of our understanding; the more we understand, the more we will see... like scaling a mountain).

Where Does Real and Sustained Joy or Fulfillment Come From?

- Spending your life in pursuits that realize your potential and awaken your talents (growing)

- Transcending fears and letting go of limiting beliefs

- Achieving worthy goals and creating success on our own terms (rather than according to the definition of success of those around us)

- Rich and meaningful relationships

- Elevating in self-knowledge

- Adding value to others (from clients and co-workers to people in our communities)

- Making a positive difference and having an impact on the world around you

So yes, own things (it's a very human hunger). Get the shiny objects of allure that call out for your attention. And once you own them, enjoy them. But don't let them own you. Possess them. But don't be possessed by them.

**COMMIT TO DOING
PROJECTS THAT
TERRIFY YOU +
SHIFTING FROM
ACCEPTING
GOOD WORK FROM
YOURSELF TO
DEMANDING
LEGENDARY
PRODUCTION
FROM YOURSELF.**

MY ACTION MASTERY TOOL

What I'm Grateful for Today:

Where I will Pursue Mastery Today:

What I Learned Today:

33

GREATNESS BY EVOLUTION VERSUS REVOLUTION

Most training programs don't have a lasting impact. Most seminars provoke only micro-change. Most inspirational or leadership books get us excited only until we wake up the next morning and reality intrudes on our idealistic vision.

Why does this all happen? Because too many training programs, seminars and books are attempting to cause a revolution rather than nurture an evolution. Big idea there.

If you go to a seminar and hear a ton of lessons that you know will take your career and your life to your NLG (Next Level of Greatness; please forgive my acronyms... just a mood I'm in these days. Let's hope it will pass), it's easy to get caught up in 'revolution mode'.

There's so much to transform and so little time to do it in.

And human beings don't like to change (it scares us). So we drift into overwhelm. And we don't even start.

I suggest to you that there's a better way to get to world-class within the important areas of your life: evolution.

Small, baby steps. Daily and continuous micro improvements. Steady and consistent elevations in the way you work, lead and live.

My dad always said slow and steady wins the race.

Every dream started off small and grew step by step.

One hundred and twenty years ago, at Jacobs Pharmacy, a customer paid Dr. John Stith Pemberton, a local pharmacist, five cents for his sugar-in-a-glas concoction that you may have heard of (it's called Coca-Cola and is enjoyed more than a billion times a day around the world).

Evolution versus revolution.

Sam Walton, the founder of Wal-Mart, started with a single store and didn't even get to the big box idea until he was in business for about thirty years.

Evolution, not revolution.

The Everest climbers don't jump up to the summit. No, they climb it bit by bit.

Evolution, not... You get my point.

Day by day, step by step, you can move towards your own personal mountaintop. You (and your organization) really can be, do and have a lot more than you've ever imagined. The life you are living today can be radically different from the life you can have three or six months from now.

I see it happen all the time with my clients. And you'll get to the professional and personal greatness you deserve through an evolution, not through a revolution.

ON OUR ENTRANCE
INTO THE WORLD,
WE HAVE NOTHING.
AND ON OUR EXIT,
WE TAKE NOTHING.
SO WHY
WORRY
SO MUCH
ABOUT THINGS?
GROW YOUR
CRAFT.
SCALE YOUR
CHARACTER.
AND SERVE
THE WORLD.

What I'm Grateful for Today:

_____

_____

_____

_____

_____

Where I will Pursue Mastery Today:

_____

_____

_____

_____

_____

What I Learned Today:

_____

_____

_____

_____

_____

34

YOU FIND
WHAT YOU SEEK

Every second you spend thinking about what you don't want
in your life is a second denying focus and energy from getting
what you do want.

Every minute you worry about what's not working is a
minute drawn away from creating what will work.

And every hour spent reflecting on the disappointments
of the past is an hour stolen from seeing the possibilities that
your future holds.

What I've discovered in my own life is that I see more of
what I look for. Clarity precedes mastery (big idea there) and
the more clearly I look for what I want, the more powerfully I
generate that result in my life.

By setting clear goals in the important areas, I see more

of what I'm searching for. By looking for the best in others, I generally find it.

And by looking for the good things in my life and expressing gratitude for my blessings (rather than thinking about any problems), I see more of what's good.

Your thinking will create your reality. Your thoughts form your world? Why? Because you will never act against your thinking. Every action is the offspring of a thought. And your actions create the professional and personal life you find yourself in today.

WHEN YOUR VISION BECOMES YOUR MISSION, YOUR BUSINESS WILL BECOME A MOVEMENT.

What I'm Grateful for Today:

Where I will Pursue Mastery Today:

What I Learned Today:

35

CONVERSATIONS WITH ECCENTRICS

Only leaders (and we all can Lead Without Title) who are willing to think differently can out-innovate everyone around them. Thinking the same thoughts produces the same results. Leadership is all about being the Brave Creative out in front in your marketspace (and your career) versus doing things the way everyone else does them.

Business doesn't need more copycats. Business needs more Dreamers.

Apple came up with the gorgeous (and now ubiquitous iPod). Now there are so many products with the letter "i" in front of it, I've lost track. Too much copying. Not enough leading.

A well-respected business leader told me about a CEO who did something that made me smile. He hired a young wonderkid fresh out of business school – a kid who was not only brilliant, but thought differently, and wasn't afraid to voice his eccentric thoughts. The mandate of the new hire? Sit on the company's management team and consistently challenge ideas that fostered the status quo. This man was paid to push the envelope. To evangelize innovation. To make things better by being unorthodox in a world where most of us are afraid to leave the crowd.

So today, have conversations with people who are Originals. Strive to leave the Safe Harbor of the Known. Make things better. Play bigger. And dream.

THE GREAT VICTORY OF SUCCESS IS BEING TRUE TO THE GRANDEST VISION OF YOUR BIGGEST LIFE.

What I'm Grateful for Today:

_____

_____

_____

_____

_____

_____

Where I will Pursue Mastery Today:

_____

_____

_____

_____

_____

What I Learned Today:

_____

_____

_____

_____

_____

36

NEXT-LEVEL LISTENING

People ache for great listening. Do you give it to them? I so passionately believe that one of the single best things you can do to get your relationships (both professional and personal) to world-class is to become alarmingly good at listening. Yup, alarmingly good is the standard I'm pressing you to reach.

As a young lawyer, I worked with a senior litigator who was just 'insanely great' (Steve Jobs' term) at making people feel heard. It wasn't forced. It wasn't faked. It wasn't artificial. Just a truckload of masterful, heartfelt listening every time I was with him. And guess what, that was the best professional relationship I had at that office. I'd do anything for him. He had my respect. And my loyalty. And my outright friendship. Because I knew (versus believed) he cared.

Listening's like that. Seems like simple stuff, this listening business. But it's outrageously hard in a world where we can be so self-centered. And in a world where we all suffer from collective ADD. So hard to focus. So hard to concentrate. So hard to listen.

But no organization can get to extraordinary without excited, engaged and enthusiastic people. And no human being can ever find authentic success without the help of people.

And people need listening. They crave it. Hunger for it. More than you may imagine.

Oh, the way it feels when someone gives you the listening you need. It's so very rare, isn't it? And yet so exceptionally powerful.

I know you want to reach your mountaintop. I know you know you've been enlisted for greatness. I know you are one of the rare breed that is doing special things.

And one of the most special of all is being a brilliant listener.

Get to your Next Level of Listening. Master that art. It'll rock your world.

TO LEAD IS
TO AFFIRM THE
GREATNESS
WITHIN
EVERYONE
YOU MEET TODAY.

What I'm Grateful for Today:

Where I will Pursue Mastery Today:

What I Learned Today:

37

READY-MADE GREATNESS

Michelangelo was asked how he created his masterpieces.
He replied that he simply saw the works of art embedded
within the slabs of marble and then set about chipping away at
everything that wasn't of that work of art. Which brings me to
you. And your ready-made greatness.

Just maybe your job is not to become someone other than
who you currently are. Just maybe the Main Aim is to access
and remember and reconnect with the best that already resides
within you. In this very moment. Right here. Right now.

And how can you recall your personal greatness?

By starting the process of chipping away everything that is
not truly you. The fears you have picked up. The limiting beliefs
you have accumulated. The false assumptions that divorce you

from your most authentic – and staggeringly brilliant – self.

Self-remembering (and personal leadership) is a journey. Took you many years to forget the personal greatness that you once knew as a kid (before the disappointments and negativity of the world began to blind you to the truth of your bigness). You may have been thinking you have been designed for mediocrity for 30 or 40 or 50 years. So that reconnection with your best won't happen in a week.

But chip away, bit by bit, at everything that is not that work of art, day by day. You know that small, daily improvements stack into massive results over time (that idea just might transform your life so please let it linger).

The difference between a remarkable life and a mediocre one is not nearly as large as you might imagine. Nope, we all pretty much start out with the same raw stuff. Most of us are cut from the same cloth. We can all be heroes if we choose. And it just isn't that hard.

Greatness comes by doing a few small and smart things each and every day. Comes from taking little steps, consistently. Comes from a making a few small chips against everything in your professional and personal life that is ordinary, so that a day eventually arrives when all that's left is The Extraordinary. Just something to think about, from a man who wants you to shine.

A DREAM WITHOUT DEVOTION IS A FANTASY, NOT REALITY.

What I'm Grateful for Today:

_____

_____

_____

_____

_____

Where I will Pursue Mastery Today:

_____

_____

_____

_____

_____

What I Learned Today:

_____

_____

_____

_____

_____

38

THE BRILLIANCE OF DIVERSITY

Imagine living in a world where every movie you see has the same story line. Imagine if the only choice of drink was water and the only flavor of ice cream was chocolate (okay, maybe that one wouldn't be so bad). Imagine that every conversation with every person made the same point.

And imagine that every day had the same ending and that every thought reflected the same idea. There's a point I'm getting to. Please stay with me.

When I go to organizations to help inspire, develop and elevate employees so they play at world-class levels (and I've been crisscrossing this planet on this Leadership Crusade for nearly ten years now), I often see mission statements espousing a respect for diversity. "We at ClientCo value differences and cherish diversity." And most of the companies I work with actually do. But here's my question: do you?

Do you really get the brilliance of diversity? When you really think about it, it's the people who see the world through a different set of lenses that actually serve to stretch your thinking, and provoke new understanding (and provoke they do). Sure, they irritate you. They drive you crazy. Because they are not like you. But may I suggest that behind your irritation is the emotion of fear (big idea there). Not the terror of the darkness type of fear. More a fear of the unknown or a fear of having to leave the Safe Harbor of the Known (the worldview that you've had your whole life) and maybe see a new way of seeing things. No one likes to leave the shores of the home they know. Always brings up fear. Scary? Yes. For your ultimate growth and good? Absolutely.

Never run away from what will help you grow and step into your greatness, no matter how uncomfortable it makes you feel (that's where courage and your natural bravery needs to be called into service).

Yup, diversity helps us in ways we cannot fathom. Makes us better (by a lot). Those different people with different perspectives, different skin colors and different languages can equip you with your MILs (Most Important Lessons).

People and experiences that are different offer you the gorgeous opportunity to rethink the assumptions and closely held opinions you have lived your life under.

It takes a ton of outright courage to open your mind, as well as your heart, and listen to what they tell you. Uber-uncomfortable to think that you might not be right; the way you see the world (or whatever) just might be flawed in some way. Or that there may be a better way (of thinking or behaving or working or living).

But unless you are willing to empty the cup that is full, no more can enter. And you just might miss out on your greatest possibilities. And your best life.

TAKERS DON'T INSPIRE THE WORLD. GIVERS DO.

What I'm Grateful for Today:

_____

_____

_____

_____

_____

_____

Where I will Pursue Mastery Today:

_____

_____

_____

_____

_____

_____

What I Learned Today:

_____

_____

_____

_____

_____

_____

39

JIM DONALD
GETS IT

You can have your excuses or you can have your results, but you can't have both. It's easy to find excuses not to build relationships and be one of those brilliant souls who masterfully connects with human beings – a mile-long to-do list, missed deadlines and forest fires to put out. Who has the time to engage in face to face conversations or build rich bonds with the people we work with (or serve)? Jim Donald does.

Donald is the CEO of a little coffee company that started in Pike's Place Market in Seattle. He's a pretty busy guy too. Tons of to-dos and places to be.

Full schedule like you and me. But he finds time to put people first. He gets the fact that the way you treat your people is the way they'll treat your customers. He understands that when people feel great about themselves, they do great work.

Oh, you may have heard about the company he runs. It's called Starbucks.

This guy's amazing.

According to the latest issue of *Fortune*, on a good day, he personally signs 500 birthday cards for his employees and spends 45% of his time traveling to Starbucks stores.

And when he gets there, guess what he does?

He puts on an apron and works shoulder to shoulder with the baristas. He engages his people in conversations, evangelizes his message and reinforces his vision. He builds culture and makes his 'partners' feel special. He puts his people first and so, they help him win.

SUCCESS WITHOUT SERVICE IS AN EMPTY VICTORY.

What I'm Grateful for Today:

Where I will Pursue Mastery Today:

What I Learned Today:

40

LEAD LIKE ISSY

Isadore Sharpe started a little company called The Four Seasons with a single little hotel in 1961. He made deals based on a handshake; he spoke his truth and kept his word. He did great work and offered great value.

Well, good things happen to people who do good things (key thought to remember).

The Four Seasons, now one of the most successful hotel chains, recently received purchase offers from the likes of Bill Gates and other heavy-hitters. Friends and colleagues of Issy Sharpe said things like, "He deserves all the great things happening to him". He stands to make hundreds of millions. His reputation continues to soar. A fitting way to tie up his Cinderella Story.

Lessons I took away from these recent events:

1. **Stay true to your vision or dream:** There's something to be said for just staying at what you are trying to achieve well past the point everyone else gives up. Life rewards the (unreasonably) devoted.

2. **Stay true to your values:** In a world of fast-buck artists and people playing the short-game, Issy took the long-view; he built high-trust relationships. He protected his brand; underpromised and overdelivered. He didn't care if others were unethical, and stayed true to himself.

3. **The little things amount to big things:** Issy's dream started small. But he tended to it daily. Small daily elevations compound into massive results over time. Remember that success comes via those daily '1% Wins'.

So model Issy, no matter what work you're doing today. Because leadership is all about Leading Where You're Planted. And it's not about the size of you're title, but the depth of your commitment.

YOUR HABITS ARE PRISTINE REFLECTIONS OF YOUR VALUES.

What I'm Grateful for Today:

_____

_____

_____

_____

_____

_____

Where I will Pursue Mastery Today:

_____

_____

_____

_____

_____

_____

What I Learned Today:

_____

_____

_____

_____

_____

_____

41

BE A
FINISHER

Talk is cheap. Actions speak. Doesn't matter what you start.

It's brilliant that you have the courage to take that first step (nothing changes until you change). But what's the point of starting if you don't finish?

Leadership and greatness comes to those who follow-through; who stand for near-flawless execution; who stay with a projector, a pursuit or an idea with the tenacity of a pit bull until the thing gets done, beautifully.

So right here, right now, reach deep into your heart. And commit from the best place that inhabits you – to finish the important things you start.

Because anyone can take the first step. But only the remarkable ones stay on the path until they complete the 1000th one.

YOU CAN'T WIN IF YOU DON'T BEGIN.

What I'm Grateful for Today:

_____

_____

_____

_____

_____

_____

Where I will Pursue Mastery Today:

_____

_____

_____

_____

_____

What I Learned Today:

_____

_____

_____

_____

_____

_____

42

CARLY GETS IT

You know how fiercely I believe that every dream starts small and nothing moves forward until you do. Just read about former Hewlett-Packard CEO, Carly Fiorina. Her memoir is called *Tough Choices*. She actually did a quick stint as a typist at HP at the beginning of her career. But she always wanted to be great and stood for excellence (a guy in a car with a license plate that said 'V Best' drove by me today as I drove my kids to school; my guess is he stands for the same thing).

One of her big insights:

"Don't think about the next job, focus on doing the best with the job you have. Learn everything you can from everyone you can. Focus on the possibilities of each job, not the limitations."

Could I suggest that we read that advice a few times to really integrate it?

Because it's good.

No, actually, it's superb.

It's so easy to tell everyone around you that you'll be best in class when you get the position you've been aching for. It's so easy to say you'll innovate or raise the bar or step up to remarkable once you receive the title you've aimed at. It's so easy to advertise that you'll be an A player when you get to where you're going.

But we get what we give.

Not later, but now.

And if not now, then when?

WHY FOLLOW THE CROWD WHEN YOU CAN LISTEN TO YOURSELF?

What I'm Grateful for Today:

_____

_____

_____

_____

_____

_____

Where I will Pursue Mastery Today:

_____

_____

_____

_____

_____

_____

What I Learned Today:

_____

_____

_____

_____

_____

_____

43

THE DREAM
CATCHER

You may not know how powerful you are.

Big Idea: Every one of us has so many more choices than
we can currently see. Remember, we see the world not as it is,
but as we are.

Most of us see through the eyes of our fears, our limiting
beliefs and our false assumptions. That's a really important
point there.

As you begin to walk to your fears, you realize that they
were mostly hallucinations – self-created illusions that kept
you small. As you think about your limiting beliefs, you'll see
that they are not the truth, but the opinions you adopted from
the chattering voices around you. And as you question your
assumptions, you'll realize that so many of them are borne of

fantasy. They are not real. Nope, not at all. Most of the things we are afraid will happen, never do. Something to think about.

Today, I want to offer you the words of James Allen who wrote a superb little book called *As a Man Thinketh* many years ago.

They will help you enormously as you catch your dreams and step up to the poetic possibilities your life is meant to be:

"Of all of the beautiful truths pertaining to the soul which have been restored and brought to light in this age, none is more gladdening and fruitful of divine promise and confidence than this – that you are the master of your thought, the molder of your character, and the maker and shaper of condition, environment and destiny."

THE FEARS WE DON'T FACE BECOME OUR LIMITS. THE OPPORTUNITIES WE DON'T SEIZE BECOME OUR WALLS.

What I'm Grateful for Today:

_____

_____

_____

_____

_____

_____

_____

Where I will Pursue Mastery Today:

_____

_____

_____

_____

_____

_____

What I Learned Today:

_____

_____

_____

_____

_____

_____

44

SUCCESS VIA SIMPLICITY

Love what the co-founder of Google recently said: **"Success will come from simplicity."**

I invite you to really go deep into his words. They are enormously powerful. Success via simplicity – a great insight.

Most people, in business and within their personal lives move towards complexity. More to-dos. More projects. More products. More meetings. More possessions. More goals.

The best, I suggest to you, is to move in the opposite direction.

They try and make their business models leaner and more focused. They do fewer, but smarter things. They get wildly focused and wonderfully lean. And they most definitely run from trying to be all things to all people.

Because real genius lives in simplicity.

YOUR 'I CAN' IS MORE IMPORTANT THAN YOUR IQ.

What I'm Grateful for Today:

_____

_____

_____

_____

_____

Where I will Pursue Mastery Today:

_____

_____

_____

_____

_____

What I Learned Today:

_____

_____

_____

_____

_____

45

LEARN AT INTERSECTIONS

Simple idea with powerful consequences:
  Everyone who intersects your life knows something you don't.
  To get to world-class, don't miss any opportunity to leverage the learning, insights and experiences of the people you meet.
  Because we really do become our conversations.

VICTIMS LOVE ENTERTAINMENT. LEADERS LOVE EDUCATION.

What I'm Grateful for Today:

Where I will Pursue Mastery Today:

What I Learned Today:

46

BE LIKE PETER
(DRUCKER)

The thing I like about famous management guru, Peter Drucker's thinking is that he didn't just put out good ideas – he offered great Insights. Ideas really are a dime a dozen. We all get smart ideas. But to win, get to world-class or to make your mark, something more is needed. Insight. Brilliant ones actually.

Like this one: "Get Good or Get Out."

Seems so obvious.

But to me, when you go down to the roots of it, it's revolutionary.

See, the only way a business can become great is to be BIW: Best in the World at what you do.

Well, most businesses, and people, are so busy doing so many things that they forget that focus creates mastery. You just can't help but get better (and eventually brilliant) if you pick a few things (even better, just One Big Thing) to concentrate on and then spend the rest of your days in specialization.

"Get Good or Get Out."

Why play in a space you can't win in?

Why waste your time?

Instead, figure out your Big Bets.

Get to know what you're really good at. And then have the force of will to go there.

You'll be dazzled by the rewards.

THE MARKETPLACE
REWARDS
MASTERY.
PEOPLE
ALWAYS
PAY FOR
THE BEST.

What I'm Grateful for Today:

Where I will Pursue Mastery Today:

What I Learned Today:

47

LEVERAGE HARD RELATIONSHIPS

Big Idea: Your most challenging relationship carries with it the seeds of your greatest growth. The relationship that tests, frustrates or irritates you the most, is actually one of your greatest blessings.

Why?

Because it reveals to you the very beliefs, fears and false assumptions that most limit you. Get that and you can step into your NLG: Next Level of Greatness.

What I'm suggesting to you is that (if you choose to do so) you can leverage your hardest relationship into your greatest success.

The people you can't stand can actually transform your life. And help you become happier, healthier and more successful.

Unbelievable, isn't it?

The best in business and in life use that aggravating relationship (the one that presses all their buttons and makes them want to scream) to discover what's keeping them small. They ask themselves what the beliefs they are running are, that allow them to get so provoked by this person. They have the outright bravery to go deep and see the fears that person triggers versus making it all about the other person being wrong or incompetent or ignorant or whatever other labels we generally use to avoid looking in the mirror and assuming personal responsibility. And the great ones use what they learn to build greater self-awareness, authentic power and personal understanding.

Please remember that as you become a more extraordinary human being, every element of your outer world must change accordingly. It just has to.

So the more remarkable you become, the more remarkable will be the professional and personal life you'll create.

Inner improvements create outer ones.

No two people see the world in precisely the same way. How could we, as each of us have had different experiences on the journey through our days?

What a word or an event means to you might mean something totally different to me. What a gorgeous opportunity, then, is the intersection of two people who view the world differently. We can embrace that connection to learn, grow and elevate the very people we are. And the growth and inner expansion that we experience from that one challenging relationship will change the way we relate in every other relationship.

Improve the way you show up in one relationship and you'll

improve the way you show up in every other relationship (from your teammates and customers at work to the people you love at home). Exciting, no?

Not only that, but it will change who we are. We will never be the same as we stretch and expand with what we discover in that difficult interaction. We will be stronger, wiser, bigger and better. And that'll revolutionize everything. Forever.

YOU CAN MAKE IT ALL ABOUT YOU. OR YOU CAN CHANGE THE WORLD. YOU CAN'T DO BOTH.

What I'm Grateful for Today:

_____

_____

_____

_____

_____

_____

Where I will Pursue Mastery Today:

_____

_____

_____

_____

_____

_____

What I Learned Today:

_____

_____

_____

_____

_____

_____

48

THE
ONE LEAP

It's stunningly interesting to me how we have the power to, over the hours of this very day, make a decision, choice or commitment that can transform our professional as well as our personal lives forever.

This day can be the first day of your new life. The day that changes everything; the day you stopped playing small and stood up for the poetic possibilities your life was meant to have. I get excited just thinking about that. Seriously.

So my question to you is a simple one: what one leap could you make today that, if you made it, would change the game? What one Bold Step could you take that would radically alter the way you think, feel and behave?

What New Move could you step into that would lift

you into the realm of extraordinary, remarkable, world-class?

Now, today, why not take that step?

There will never be a perfect time to be the greatest you.

Actually, there will never be a better time than today to make the improvements you need, to be the leader and human being that you've always dreamed of being.

So why wait? Do It Now.

WE CREATE THAT WHICH WE FEAR. ALL BEHAVIOUR IS A DEMONSTRATION OF OUR PSYCHOLOGY. SO GET TO WORK ON ACKNOWLEDGING AND THEN RELEASING YOUR FEAR.

What I'm Grateful for Today:

Where I will Pursue Mastery Today:

What I Learned Today:

49

ACHIEVING LONGEVITY AND GREATNESS IN BUSINESS

In my leadership development work with companies like IBM, FedEx and Nike, and as an executive coach to many of the superstars in business, I have been blessed to have been able to closely observe the traits that the best use to get better – and achieve longevity within their careers and within themselves.

Here are some of their personal practices for sustainability:

1. **They have a lust for learning:** There is a cure for anti-aging that actually works: it's called lifelong learning. To ABL (Always Be Learning) is to stay young forever. The best in business have boundless curiosity and open minds. And this allows them to work and live with a

childlike sense of wonder as well as access world-class levels of creativity that fuels their professional success. They read constantly. They listen to books on CD. And they understand that everyone they meet knows at least one thing that they don't. So they ask good questions (like any good leader). In this world of dazzling change and stunning opportunity, ideas are the commodity of success. And a passion for learning makes you a human idea factory.

2. **They devote to NSI:** A mantra of many world-class businesspeople is Never Stop Improving. As I've written in my book *The Greatness Guide*, nothing fails like success. Success is seductive. It can make one complacent, inefficient and stale. Too often, once a person (as well as an organization) becomes successful, the very things that created that success get neglected. The best businesspeople have a hunger to make their todays better than their yesterdays. They have a staggeringly large appetite for pushing the envelope. They stretch their personal frontiers by taking risks, by running to their fears and by improving every area of their lives. Relentlessly. This serves to keep them young at heart. And at the cutting edge for years.

3. **They know that health is wealth:** At a leadership seminar I delivered in Delhi to executives, a participant handed me a piece of paper that said: "Health is the crown on the well man's head that only the ill man can see." Big idea. We take our health for granted until we lose it. And if we do, we spend all our time trying to get it back. It's fascinating to me how, while we are young,

we are willing to sacrifice our health for wealth and yet, when we grow old, we become willing to give up all of our accumulated wealth for one day of good health. Getting into world-class physical condition will make you more creative, energetic, focused and happy. Make that leap today.

4. **They find a cause:** In *The Greatness Guide,* I wrote that the real secret to immortality and longevity is to find a cause that's larger than yourself and then have the courage to donate your life to it. That cause might be being an extraordinary leader who creates an extraordinary organization that creates extraordinary value for it's customers. That cause might be to become a person devoted to leaving everyone you meet better than you found them. That cause might mean being a manager that develops the highest potential of his people and evokes their greatness.

When I was growing up, my dad shared an Indian saying with me that still lives within my imagination: "When you were born, you cried while the world rejoiced. Live your life in such a way that when you die, the world cries while you rejoice."

DON'T ASK FOR RESPECT. EARN IT.

What I'm Grateful for Today:

Where I will Pursue Mastery Today:

What I Learned Today:

50

FOCUS TO WIN

In *The Greatness Guide* I share a simple formula for genius: focus plus time equals mastery. Please think about that. What you concentrate on, you cannot help but become great at. The more you focus, the better you get.

Focus on being superb at what you do and, over time, you will be known as remarkable.

Focus on your health and, of course, in time, it will get to splendid.

Focus on developing your kids and you cannot be denied having great kids.

Focus on your inner world and people will eventually call you wise.

Focus. Focus. Focus. On your burning priorities.

Say no to everything else. Life's short. You only get one shot at great. Will you accept the Call? Or let the opportunity slide by you. Like too many amongst us.

SMARTER TO FOCUS ON QUALITY VERSUS SPEED.

What I'm Grateful for Today:

_____

_____

_____

_____

_____

Where I will Pursue Mastery Today:

_____

_____

_____

_____

_____

What I Learned Today:

_____

_____

_____

_____

_____

51

BUILD YOUR POWER

Life's counter-intuitive. The things that we most resist, carry the seeds of our greatness.

The stuff that makes us feel uncomfortable makes us stronger. And the things that are hard to do help us get to our authentic power. Difficult is Good.

Wowing a customer when you just can't smile another smile makes you more powerful. Being honest when it's easy to lie builds your character. Being excellent on a job or a project or a task when no one's watching grows self-respect, inner resolve and personal honor. The hard stuff is the great stuff.

It's the very building blocks of a brilliant life.

The easy road gets you to a place called disappointment and regret. Please trust me on that: I spend my life traveling the planet and working with people and companies, so my ear's close to the ground. Doing what you know you are called to do is the secret of success, mastery and inner peace.

As my friend Nido Qubein once said: "The price of discipline is less than the pain of regret." I wish I'd said that!

FEAR
ONLY BECOMES
POWERFUL
WHEN YOU
GIVE IT
YOUR POWER.
OWN
YOUR
BRAVERY
TODAY.

What I'm Grateful for Today:

_____

_____

_____

_____

_____

_____

Where I will Pursue Mastery Today:

_____

_____

_____

_____

_____

What I Learned Today:

_____

_____

_____

_____

_____

52

HOW BIG ARE YOUR SHOES?

Just read a Harley Davidson ad. The main line:

> "Leave Behind Shoes
> No Man Can Fill."

Love it.

How big a life are you living? How bold a dream are you dreaming?

How remarkable a person are you becoming?

And, how large a footprint will you leave behind, such that the generations who will follow you will know that you've been here? And made your mark.

LIVE YOUR LIFE AS AN EXAMPLE OF POSSIBILITY.

What I'm Grateful for Today:

Where I will Pursue Mastery Today:

What I Learned Today:

53

THE GIANT LEAP

Small steps are big steps. Little decisions can, over time, cause stunningly wonderful results. Tiny changes lead to real and sustained transformation. It's all about evolution rather than revolution. I know you know that.

It's so exciting to me to think that, this very day, can serve as a springboard to an extraordinary professional and personal life. One decision you make over the coming hours could be the giant leap that launches a tidal wave of greatness that leads you to a place well above your boldest dreams. Remarkable, isn't it, this thing called choice? And everyone of us can exercise it. Yes, every single one of us.

No decision is unimportant. Every action leads to a reaction. Each move we make creates a consequence and ripples across our destiny. Getting up earlier when you feel like sleeping is the giant leap that begins a new habit called early rising. Coming up with a better way to think, feel or behave at work is the giant leap that creates a new inner pathway called excellence and mastery. Treating people with more respect, kindness and understanding is the giant leap that will soon install a routine called humanity.

That little first step sends a clear signal to life that you want to change and have the courage to make the first move.

The first move is always the hardest.

Everything's easier after that.

Step by step, changing and elevating your game gets easier. You become more confident. The new habits and internal pathways become more familiar. And you, almost invisibly, become greater. And more brilliant. And more of the person you were born to be. Told you, it's exciting!

WHEN WE GIVE UP ON OUR DREAMS, WE DIE WHILE STILL ALIVE.

What I'm Grateful for Today:

_____

_____

_____

_____

_____

Where I will Pursue Mastery Today:

_____

_____

_____

_____

_____

What I Learned Today:

_____

_____

_____

_____

_____

54

A GOOD CEO

Just read a letter excerpted in Fast Company. From John Mackey, the CEO of Whole Foods. He writes:

"The tremendous success of Whole Foods Market has provided me with far more money than is necessary for my financial security or personal happiness... I am now 53 years old and I have reached a place in my life where I no longer want to work for money, but simply for the joy of work itself and to better answer the call to service that I feel so clearly in my own heart. Beginning on January 1, 2007, my salary will be reduced to $1..."

There's a sea change in the corporate world. So many people want to be a part of a good company. Ethics are back.

Creating rich value for customers is back. Being good is back.

What will you do today to grow this revolution?

YOUR PAIN HAS
PURIFIED
YOU. YOUR
STUMBLES HAVE
STRENGTHENED
YOU. YOUR
FAILURE HAS
FORTIFIED
YOU.

What I'm Grateful for Today:

_____

_____

_____

_____

_____

_____

Where I will Pursue Mastery Today:

_____

_____

_____

_____

_____

_____

What I Learned Today:

_____

_____

_____

_____

_____

_____

55

IT'S ALL ABOUT GROWTH

Just read a quote that provoked me: "Growth is the only evidence of life." Pretty smart words. They came from John Henry Newman.

You know I adore the whole notion of growth. To me, that's why were here. To grow and expand through the work we do, the actions we take and the lives we lead (don't just live your life, lead it).

Growth matters. It's what ultimately makes us feel fulfilled. It energizes us (even when it's uncomfortable, and most growth is). Makes us who we truly are.

THE JOB OF THE LEADER IS TO GROW MORE LEADERS.

What I'm Grateful for Today:

_____

_____

_____

_____

_____

_____

Where I will Pursue Mastery Today:

_____

_____

_____

_____

_____

_____

What I Learned Today:

_____

_____

_____

_____

_____

_____

56

RESPECT
YOU

It doesn't matter what other people think of you. All that
matters is what you think of you.

We lose so much energy worrying about the opinions of
others, wanting to be liked.

Leadership and personal mastery is about rising above
social approval – to self approval.

Respect you. So long as you are living by your values, being
authentic, running your own race and doing your dreams, who
cares what anyone else thinks, feels or says about you?

As I wrote in *The Greatness Guide*: "Leadership isn't a
popularity contest."

It's about doing what's right.

YOU'LL NEVER BE A BETTER LEADER THAN YOU ARE A PERSON.

What I'm Grateful for Today:

Where I will Pursue Mastery Today:

What I Learned Today:

57

LESS TALK, MORE DO

Too many people talk too good a talk these days. Tons of empty promises. Tons of hyperbole. Tons of lofty statements that never amount to anything.

Leaders are different. They talk less and do more. I love the quiet leaders. Those silent souls who underpromise and overdeliver.

The Merchants of Wow amongst us who know that a person's word is their bond. And that every promise kept builds credibility – the foundation of trust.

So make a commitment today to be impeccable with your word. And be a person of action. Someone who is all about generating results. Because getting great things done speaks for itself.

TO LEAD IS TO SERVE. TO HELP OTHERS IS TO WIN.

What I'm Grateful for Today:

Where I will Pursue Mastery Today:

What I Learned Today:

58

THE IMPORTANCE OF BEING REMARKABLE

Your expectations for yourself, and your life, become self-fulfilling prophecies. What you intend shapes what you become. So make a commitment, today, to be remarkable.

Live full out. Vow to be brilliant at your work. Devote to getting into world-class health. Take positive risks to grow into your greatness. Love like there's no tomorrow. And enjoy every moment.

Life's an incredible adventure. Tons of highs and lots of lows. But all of it, is precious. Gorgeous. And designed with your best interests in mind. So embrace it all.

WORLDLY SUCCESS DOES NOT GUARANTEE INNER PEACE.

What I'm Grateful for Today:

Where I will Pursue Mastery Today:

What I Learned Today:

59

PROBLEMS ARE SERVANTS

We all face challenges. It's the human condition. Everyone, on this very day, is dealing with something they wish they weren't dealing with. Some have lost a loved one. Others are facing an illness. For others, it's a money issue or some frustration at work.

Yes, it's no fun.

But just maybe every problem you encounter is an opportunity in disguise. And if you're wise to see that, you can leverage the challenge for even greater success.

In some ways, leadership is a mind game. Positive thinking is a lot more important than cynics would suggest.

The founders of Google used positive thinking to overcome their early setbacks and to stay true to their vision.

Sam Walton used positive thinking to build an empire.

And the best managers use positive thinking to help their teams see that what ordinary people view as stumbling blocks, the best amongst us see as stepping stones.

Because problems are servants. And they truly can serve you well. If you choose to let them.

FAILURE
IS FUEL FOR
SUCCESS
IF YOU
CHOOSE
SO.

What I'm Grateful for Today:

Where I will Pursue Mastery Today:

What I Learned Today:

60

NO TRY,
NO WIN

Such a simple idea: you can't win if you don't try. So often, we get a big idea. One that will get our careers to the next level. One that will get our lives to the next level. One that will really set us soaring.

But then, guess what happens next? The voice of fear takes over.

We start selling ourselves on all the reasons why we'll fail. Eventually, that beautiful, big, bold idea seems silly, unattainable and foolish. **And so we don't act. We don't even try.**

Imagine Tiger Woods wanting to win, but not even playing the tournament. Imagine the great manager wanting to lead her team to world-class, but not even showing up. Imagine the brave inventor wanting to change the world. Yet not even doing anything. Nothing happens until you move (tattoo that line on your brain cells if you really want to win). And you'll never win if you don't even try.

Enough said.

ANYONE
CAN LEAD WHEN
THE PLAN IS
WORKING.
THE BEST LEAD
WHEN THE PLAN
FALLS
APART.

What I'm Grateful for Today:

Where I will Pursue Mastery Today:

What I Learned Today:

61

HONOR IS
HIP

In this age of foul-mouthed rock stars, famous for being famous celebrities and uber-greedy CEOs who take home huge rewards while the shares of their companies hit rock bottom, there's a new way to be cool, hip and fashionable. Be honorable.

It used to be that things like honesty, giving your best at work, treating everyone you meet fairly, and being a RGP (Really Good Person) were considered boring, unsexy or bland. No longer.

In an age where too many people don't discover what leadership and life's about until it's too late, rising above the crowd to shine with a blazing sense of integrity, authenticity and rare honor is cool. Super cool. Hip.

So today, live your truth. Play your best game. Listen

to the trusted voice that resides deep within you. And show some genuine leadership – both at work and at home. People will love you for it.

And I'll think you're hip.

WHAT YOU RELEASE INTO THE WORLD IS DONATED BACK TO YOU. PUT OUT WORK THAT IS PURE POETRY ONLY.

What I'm Grateful for Today:

Where I will Pursue Mastery Today:

What I Learned Today:

62

YOU ARE AN ARTIST

Was at the Picasso museum in Barcelona a few weeks ago. The experience deeply influenced me. I saw how he was not afraid to deconstruct and then reinvent his art over the course of his life. I saw the way he dared. I saw his devotion to excellence – and being an outright original. Picasso has inspired me.

So here's what I think. At work each day, we are all artists.

My brushes and paints happen to be my words. My canvas is my books and the audiences I have the privilege to share my leadership message with.

But I'm an artist. I honestly feel that.

I create. I express. I provoke. And so can you.

Each day you step into the place where you work, you have the opportunity to nurture, and awaken, the artist that inhabits you.

We all have a core craving to express who we are and to create something special. Part of being human. I encourage you to satisfy that urge by being the Picasso of Human Resources or the Dali of Sales. Be the Renoir of Real Estate or the Michelangelo of Medicine.

Step out into the world each day and create your masterpiece. The world will be better for it.

ICONS
DON'T RETIRE.
THEY LOVE THEIR
CRAFT
TOO MUCH.

What I'm Grateful for Today:

_____

_____

_____

_____

_____

_____

Where I will Pursue Mastery Today:

_____

_____

_____

_____

_____

_____

What I Learned Today:

_____

_____

_____

_____

_____

_____

63

GRATITUDE FOR THE GOOD

Gratitude is a beautiful thing. It makes the recipient feel better. It makes the sender feel great.

In my journal, I often express gratitude to the people who elevate, influence and inspire me. On crisp white pages, I honor my kids for all the gifts they have brought to my life (I wish I could be half as amazing as them).

I celebrate the musicians who fill me with joy, people like Dave Matthews and Shakira and Zucchero and Nusrat Fateh Ali Khan as well as bands like the Red Hot Chilli Peppers, U2, Mana Mana and Piero Pelu. Love them all.

I appreciate my teammates who leave their homes each morning to help me share my message with people and organizations around the world ready to reach world-class.

And I thank those who have believed in me and helped me along the way.

We all have a lot more blessings in our life than we know.

It's human nature to focus on what's not working rather than to embrace all that is.

No matter how good, or bad, your life looks at this very moment, there really is so much (and so many people) you can be thankful for.

And gratitude begets gratitude. The more good things you see, the more good things you see.

TWO MAGIC WORDS?
"THANK YOU".
THEY DISPLAY
YOUR GRATITUDE.
THEY REVEAL
YOUR APPRECIATION.
THEY HONOR
THE ONE WHO
HAS BEEN
HELPFUL.

What I'm Grateful for Today:

Where I will Pursue Mastery Today:

What I Learned Today:

64

READ
STRANGE STUFF

I was reading a *Rolling Stone* magazine this morning. One of the best business magazines I read. "But *Rolling Stone* is a music magazine," you remind me. Exactly.

I often get my best business ideas from non-business magazines. Business magazines often share 'status quo' concepts and interview CEOs with an MBA who speak the same speech and think the same thoughts.

But music magazines and design magazines and travel magazines share the worldview of people who think differently.

And those are the ideas I want. In *Rolling Stone* there was a little piece on iTunes.

Everyone laughed at Apple and their vision not only for the iPod, but to be a leader in the music industry.

But who cares what the critics think. Leadership is about boldly trusting your instincts, chasing down your goals and doing what you think is right.

And they did.

Since 2003, they have sold over three billion songs at 99 cents each.

The business lesson? No risk, no reward.

From a music magazine.

5 MINUTES
OF LEARNING
TODAY IS
BETTER THAN
NO MINUTES
OF LEARNING
TODAY.

What I'm Grateful for Today:

_____

_____

_____

_____

_____

_____

Where I will Pursue Mastery Today:

_____

_____

_____

_____

_____

What I Learned Today:

_____

_____

_____

_____

_____

65

THE COURAGEOUS QUESTION

Companies don't get better if they fall in love with their success. The best ones never feel they are truly successful. The brilliant ones know that they can always improve. Humility is part of their cultural DNA.

Same for human beings. The Great Ones are all about NSI (Never Stop Improving). They want to improve the way they think. The way they feel. The way they behave. The way they execute. The way they communicate. The way they live.

Here's a tool you can integrate into your work and personal life today.

Throughout your day, keep asking yourself: "How can I make this better?"

Apply it to your work. Apply it to your relationships. Apply it to your self. As I wrote in *The Greatness Guide*: "Small daily improvements over time lead to stunning results."

AS YOU GROW MORE, YOU CAN SEE MORE. AS YOU KNOW MORE, YOU CAN ACHIEVE MORE.

What I'm Grateful for Today:

Where I will Pursue Mastery Today:

What I Learned Today:

66

LEADERSHIP IS ABOUT CLARITY

Just read a line by famed designer Karim Rashid: "I think we should always be looking 15 minutes ahead." I suggest we should always be thinking 15 years ahead.

Clarity precedes mastery and it's impossible to create an outcome, goal or result that you can't even see.

The best businesses I've worked with are so beautifully clear on where they're going, what their brand stands for and the type of people they want to populate their place with.

The most successful people know exactly what success means to them and what their mountains look like.

And each day, step by step, they steadily near that once-far destination.

You can too.

STOP
MANAGING YOUR
TIME.
START
MANAGING YOUR
FOCUS.

What I'm Grateful for Today:

_____
_____
_____
_____
_____

Where I will Pursue Mastery Today:

_____
_____
_____
_____
_____
_____

What I Learned Today:

_____
_____
_____
_____
_____
_____

67

SOFT IS HARD

Please don't tell me being kind, learning to listen, building out your vision and things like working on your character are soft. Nope. They are hard. And that's why so few of us do them.

Anyone can act tough.

What takes genuine power is to be open. To care about others. To learn from those around you. To be human.

Same for things like listening and vision and character-building. Getting good at those things takes a ton of courage. Why?

Because we need to develop humility and be willing to admit we are far from perfect. And that we need to change. And change is scary. Because it causes us to leave the comfort zone we have always known. And sail out into the blue oceans.

So the soft stuff is really the hard stuff. And the new model of leadership really is all about mastering the skills people in the past judged as soft. And those leaders that cling to the old ways of being will get left behind. By the leaders willing to do what's hard.

ALL CHANGE IS
HARD
AT FIRST,
MESSY
IN THE MIDDLE AND
GORGEOUS
AT THE
END...

What I'm Grateful for Today:

_____

_____

_____

_____

_____

_____

Where I will Pursue Mastery Today:

_____

_____

_____

_____

_____

What I Learned Today:

_____

_____

_____

_____

_____

_____

68

TO ACT IS
TO LEAD

As I wrote in *Who Will Cry When You Die?*, "The smallest
of actions is always better than the noblest of intentions."
Leadership is a lot more than just dreaming up a big idea. It's
about acting on them.

What separates the ordinary ones from the Great Ones is a
simple fact: the best of the best execute brilliantly around their
most vital priorities.

In a leadership presentation I just gave to BP, I called the
concept BRBO: Best Resources on Biggest Opportunities.

Leadership is, in so many ways, about getting good stuff
done.

Not started. Not in process. Done.

So today, make a decision that will revolutionize your career, life or self: never leave the site of an opportunity without doing something to seize it.

And be less about talk and more about DO.

GREAT
ACHIEVEMENT
ALWAYS
REQUIRES
GREAT
SACRIFICE.

What I'm Grateful for Today:

Where I will Pursue Mastery Today:

What I Learned Today:

69

THE BIG QUESTION

You know this but it may be valuable to remember that adversity introduces us to ourselves. We get to see what we are made of. Our strengths. And our weaknesses.

Hard times always pass, but serve us so well. To open us. Deliver wisdom. And teach us compassion and understanding. All core traits for you – a Leader Without Title.

Here's a question that may help you as you navigate change and challenge:

"What's the Lesson Here?"

Leverage your setbacks to make you more knowledgeable. Better. Wise. The best leaders do.

As I shared in *The Greatness Guide*: "He who experiences most wins."

THE SWIFTEST WAY TO HAVE A WORLDLY EMPIRE IS TO DEVELOP AN INTERIOR ONE. BEING CREATIVE, AUDACIOUS, AUTHENTIC AND LOVING MANIFESTS FORTUNES.

What I'm Grateful for Today:

Where I will Pursue Mastery Today:

What I Learned Today:

70

13
CHALLENGES

Part of the value I hope to add to you is to be a catalyst for positive change in your work and personal life. To gently push, move and challenge you. To get better. To grow more. To be great – regardless of your title or your background or your current reality.

Here Are 13 Challenges I Offer

Champion a child

Encourage a co-worker

Read a great book

Do something that frightens you

Write a Thank You note

Do something kind for a stranger

Wow a customer

Learn something new

Let go of a resentment

Do better work

Be more passionate

Speak truthfully

Stand for excellence

YOUR EXCUSES ARE NOTHING MORE THAN YOUR FEARS SEDUCING YOU. TODAY, LET THEM GO.

What I'm Grateful for Today:

Where I will Pursue Mastery Today:

What I Learned Today:

ABOUT THE AUTHOR

Robin Sharma is a globally respected humanitarian and the founder of a not-for-profit venture that helps children in need lead better lives.

Widely considered one of the world's top leadership experts, this pathblazer's clients include many Fortune 100 companies, famed billionaires, professional sports superstars, music icons and members of royalty.

Organizations that have engaged Robin Sharma to help them build employees who lead without a title, produce exceptional work and master change in these complex times include NASA, Microsoft, NIKE, GE, FedEx, HP, Starbucks, Oracle, Yale University, IBM Watson and the Young Presidents' Organization.

He is also one of the most in-demand keynote speakers in the world. To inquire about his availability for your next conference, visit robinsharma.com/speaking.

The author's #1 bestsellers, such as *The Monk Who Sold His Ferrari*, *The Greatness Guide* and *The Leader Who Had No Title*, have sold millions of copies in over 92 languages, making him one of the most broadly read writers alive today.

For more information, visit robinsharma.com

Fuel Your Rise by Reading All of Robin Sharma's Worldwide Bestsellers

Have you ever noticed that the most thoughtful, articulate, successful and graceful people you've met all have a common practice? They read everything they can get their hands on.

Whether you're at your mountaintop or just starting your climb, reading is one of the masterhabits of the great ones.

So here's a complete list of the author's internationally acclaimed books to support your ascent into peak productivity, total craft mastery and living beautifully—while you make your mark on history.

[ ] The 5 AM Club
[ ] The Monk Who Sold His Ferrari
[ ] The Greatness Guide
[ ] The Greatness Guide, Book 2
[ ] The Leader Who Had No Title
[ ] Who Will Cry When You Die?
[ ] Leadership Wisdom from The Monk Who Sold His Ferrari
[ ] Family Wisdom from The Monk Who Sold His Ferrari
[ ] Discover Your Destiny with The Monk Who Sold His Ferrari
[ ] The Secret Letters of The Monk Who Sold His Ferrari
[ ] The Mastery Manual
[ ] The Little Black Book for Stunning Success
[ ] The Saint, the Surfer, and the CEO

WHAT'S NEXT FOR YOUR HIGHEST SUCCESS?

Nothing transforms until you move. To ensure you experience real results, Robin Sharma is making available a potent online resource that will help you think like a titan and perform like a pro.

Go ahead and get full access to it before this offer ends at:

TheMentalMasteryToolkit.com